# The Music of George Lloyd

# The Music of George Lloyd

## Bruce Reader

Bruce Reader
2014

ISBN: 978-1-326-05227-0

www.classicalreviewer.co.uk

# Contents

# Preface

I first heard the music of George Lloyd when the BBC broadcast a performance of his Eighth Symphony in 1977. This led to a correspondence and eventually to a friendship that lasted for the last decade of the composer's life.

This small book is based on an article on George Lloyd's twelve symphonies written in 1999 and a talk made at the Three Spires Singers George Lloyd centenary seminar Saturday 5th October 2013 at Truro School Chapel, suitably revised and expanded.

# A Short Biography

George Walter Selwyn Lloyd was born on the 28th June 1913 in St Ives, Cornwall. His father, William Alexander Charles Lloyd, was the only son of Captain and Mrs. Walter Lloyd, R.N. of Cowesby Hall, near Thirsk.

His mother, Constance Priestley (Primrose) Rawson, was the eldest daughter of Mr and Mrs Selwyn Rawson, The Haugh End, Sowerby. Lloyd's parents were his first teachers, both of whom were amateur musicians in their own right, enabling the composer to learn the violin from a very early age.

In his boyhood, Lloyd suffered from serious bouts of rheumatic fever which kept him away from school. His education continued privately, until at the age of twelve, he was able to attend school. During his early teenage years, he received tuition in counterpoint and composition from Dr M P Conway, then organist at Chichester Cathedral. Lloyd began composing from the age of ten, one of his earliest pieces being a setting of a carol Evening Song with words written by his father.

In 1927, at the age of fourteen, Lloyd left school for an exclusively musical education with a brief spell at Trinity College of Music and then, for five years, studying the violin with the great English violinist, Albert Sammons and composition with Harry Farjeon.

Before the Second World War he wrote his first three symphonies and his first two operas, Iernin and The Serf. The premiere of the First Symphony was given in November 1932 by the Penzance Orchestra. The first professional performance followed a year later in November 1933, given by the Bournemouth Municipal Orchestra under the direction of the composer himself.

The first three movements of his Second Symphony were performed by the Eastbourne Municipal Orchestra in 1935 but it was not fully performed until 1986, then under the auspices of the BBC. The Third Symphony appeared in May 1933, and, after recommendation to the BBC by John Ireland, it received its first performance in London in 1935, again with the composer conducting.

It was Lloyd's father, an accomplished writer and poet, who wrote the libretto for Lloyd's first opera, Iernin, composed during 1934 and 1935. It was first performed by a semi-amateur company at The Pavilion in Penzance in November 1934. By chance, the Times music critic Frank Howes was on holiday in Cornwall and attended the performance. His enthusiastic review led to a professional performance the following June at The Lyceum Theatre in London where it had one of the longest runs of any British opera at that time.

Lloyd's second opera, The Serf, again with a libretto by William Lloyd received its first performance at The Royal Opera House, Covent Garden in October 1938 receiving excellent reviews.

In the summer of 1936 he visited Switzerland where he met Nancy Kathleen Juvet whom he married in 1937. The Second World War brought Lloyd's burgeoning career to a sudden halt. He enlisted in the Royal Marines and served on the Arctic convoys on the British cruiser, HMS Trinidad. It was during 1941, whilst at Scapa Flow, that Lloyd composed the ship's March HMS Trinidad. In March 1942, HMS Trinidad sailed from Seydisfiord in Iceland to protect a convoy on its way to Murmansk. Lloyd, as one of fourteen Royal Marine bandsmen, was employed in the transmitting station, deep in the bowels of the ship. This station was enclosed on either side by oil fuel tanks, and above by an armour-plated deck. Therefore, an escape route was difficult should the ship be hit below the water line. During an ill-fated skirmish, HMS Trinidad fired one last torpedo in an attempt to finish off a German destroyer; the steering mechanism on the torpedo jammed, causing the missile to turn back on itself and hit the ship.

Of the twenty men working below, only three men escaped including Lloyd. The knowledge that he had survived where many of his comrades had not, together with the physical injuries incurred by the ingestion of oil and water led to his hospitalisation, suffering from shell shock and severe depression.

Nursed by his wife, Nancy, he was eventually able to travel to her home in the mountains of Switzerland where, writing just a few bars at a time he wrote his Fourth Symphony. In 1947, the couple moved to Corcelettes on the banks of Lake Neuchatel in Switzerland. There, during a long hot summer, he wrote his Fifth Symphony.

In 1948, having recovered sufficiently, Lloyd and his wife moved back to London to live with his father. A commission was received for an opera, John Socman, for the 1951 Festival of Britain. The production was beset with problems which, together with the death of his father, led to a relapse in his health and his retreat from the musical world to run a smallholding at Ryewater, near Folke, in Dorset.

Lloyd continued to compose, rising early in the morning before the day's business. However, the musical fashion had changed with the rise of modernism. Scores were sent to the BBC, but returned, usually without being looked at.

Nevertheless, the music still flowed with three more symphonies, the Sixth in 1956, the Seventh between 1957 and 1959, and the

Eighth in 1961. These were all performed by the BBC Northern Symphony Orchestra conducted by Edward Downes in 1980, 1979 and 1977 respectively, the latter broadcast by the BBC. The 1960s brought his first three piano concertos; the first, subtitled Scapegoat, for John Ogdon and first performed by him, in 1964, with the Royal Liverpool Philharmonic Orchestra conducted by Sir Charles Groves.

1982 saw the start of a series of recordings by Edward Downes and the Philharmonia Orchestra of the Fourth, Fifth and Eighth symphonies on Richard Itter's pioneering Lyrita label.

The seventies brought two Violin Concertos and his Fourth piano concerto, together with a number of pieces for piano including The Road through Samarkand, St Anthony and the Bogside Beggar, The Aggressive Fishes, Intercom Baby, The Lily-leaf and the Grasshopper, The Transformation of that Naked Ape and Aubade for two pianos. Also written in the 1970s were two works for violin and piano, Lament, Air and Dance and the Violin Sonata.

That decade saw, not only Lloyd and his wife's move to London to pick up his musical career, but the beginnings of Lloyd's first major choral work, Pervigilium Veneris (The Vigil of Venus), a setting of an anonymous Roman poem in the original Latin text, completed in 1980, and first performed at the Royal Festival Hall on the 7th November 1989.

The 1980s brought a number of works for brass including Royal Parks, A Miniature Triptych and Diversions on a Bass Theme, many for brass band competitions. Lloyd's Tenth Symphony, also for brass, followed together with an Eleventh Symphony commissioned by the Albany Symphony Orchestra and premiered by them at the concert hall of the Troy Savings Bank in Troy, New York State with the composer conducting. Lloyd's Twelfth Symphony was the result of another Albany commission and was premiered at the same venue in 1990. Lloyd went on to become the Albany Symphony Orchestra's Music Director for the 1990 -1991 season.

Arguably Lloyd's masterpiece, A Symphonic Mass was commissioned and premiered at the Brighton Festival in 1993. It was a triumph, leading to other performances by both professional and amateur choirs. The work received critical acclaim and the recording by the same forces for Albany Records became a best seller both in the United Kingdom and abroad.

Another choral commission came from the Guildford Choral Society with A Litany, a setting of John Donne and completed in 1995. It was first performed at the Royal Festival Hall in March 1996. During 1997, Lloyd returned to the concerto form with his Cello Concerto. The concerto was completed in July 1997 but not recorded until three years after his death.

By now he was suffering from heart trouble but this did not prevent him from working on two orchestral suites from his opera, The Serf. Despite his continuing ill health his Requiem was begun in the autumn of 1997. Again, he worked at speed knowing that time was short, completing it by early 1998. It was dedicated to the memory of Diana, Princess of Wales and performed two years later, after the composer's death, as part of the Oxford Contemporary Music Festival in spring 2000.

George Lloyd died on the 3rd July 1998, after a final illness. His funeral took place at Golders Green Crematorium on Friday the 10th July 1998.

# The Music of George Lloyd

In 1913 a major event took place that would shake the world of music forever. On 29th May that year, in a brand new theatre, the Théâtre des Champs-Élysées, the Ballets Russes gave the first performance of Stravinsky's Le Sacre du Printemps or The Rite of Spring.

Just over four weeks later, on 28th June 1913, a certain George Walter Selwyn Lloyd was born in St Ives, Cornwall. It would be some twenty one years later that John Ireland would tell the young George Lloyd that he could hear in some passages of his opera, Iernin, the influence of Stravinsky's Rite of Spring. John Ireland had been to hear Iernin at the Lyceum in London several times and it was after a performance of the opera that Lloyd met him. Lloyd had started to visit Ireland at his Chelsea studio where he was introduced to many modern masterpieces. Despite Ireland's claim, Lloyd had never heard The Rite of Spring when he wrote Iernin.

Lloyd showed early promise as a composer though most of his very early works were destroyed many years later when consigned to the bonfire. One rare surviving example of Lloyd's early work is a carol written when he was only ten years of age. It had been kept by his father, William Lloyd, and produced by him for suggested inclusion in the opera John Socman. It appears in Act III where boys are singing a carol outside John Socman's house. In 1989 it was transcribed for two pianos and entitled Eventide. Later still it was transcribed for brass band under the title Evening Song.

Lloyd's first major work was his Symphony No.1 in A written in 1932 and first performed in Penzance. The Penwithian and Cornish Telegraph for 30th November 1932 reported '...the symphony is a marvellous creation...... full of life and colour...George Lloyd wishes to express his age and well has he succeeded...' Lloyd later recalled that at this first performance, after asking for more effort from the percussion, the drummer got so carried away that it was surprising that he didn't break his drum. After some revision, it was later performed by the Bournemouth Municipal Orchestra, conducted by the nineteen year old composer.

The form of the symphony is unusual in that it consists of an opening section followed by five short variations, then a short slow movement. The work finishes with a Vivace Fugato based on the opening subject. Interestingly, that arch modernist of the early 20th century, Prokofiev, used a similar structure in his Symphony No.2 in D minor from 1924/25, that of Introduction, five variations, Andante con fervore and a final Vivace, though in his work Prokofiev was influenced by the style mécanique that was popular at that time.

Lloyd's colourful orchestration and his love of brass and percussion are all apparent in this lively symphony. The composer himself has said that his intention was to avoid a long, ponderous work. Indeed, Lloyd was reacting, the same as many composers in the 1920s reacted, to the overlong symphonies of the past. Without doubt, Lloyd's first symphony was a considerable achievement for the young composer.

It was the Cornish landscape that truly inspired Lloyd's first opera Iernin (1933-34). This amazingly mature work by the twenty one year old composer is in no way a Celtic Twilight piece. You only have to dip into the opera at random to hear the strength of the vocal writing and see that Lloyd achieved his goal of letting the singers have the strength and power of the music. Certainly the orchestral brilliance is there but it is the singers that are given the lead.

The Cornishman and Cornish Telegraph reported 'Scenes of great dramatic intensity and moments of lyricism are embodied in the Cornish grand opera, Iernin, which was produced for the first time at the Pavilion, Penzance on Monday night.'

Elsewhere in the newspaper it was reported that 'A sharp, though brief, thunderstorm was general throughout West Cornwall on Monday night. The storm was at its worst over the coast. St Ives, which experienced the worst thunderstorm for many years, was like a town under bombardment. Houses shook and many people were terrified.'
Had the thunderstorm been active during the performance of Iernin when, towards the end of Act III Iernin is returned to stone amidst a furious storm?

Two further symphonies followed; the Second Symphony was written over two months during 1933 and the first three movements performed by the Eastbourne Municipal Orchestra, again conducted by the composer. After revision in 1982, the Symphony was given its first complete performance by the BBC Philharmonic Orchestra conducted by the composer. This performance was followed by a recording.

The Symphony opens with a lively Con brio, followed by a heartfelt Largo. This is the heart of the symphony with the young composer displaying more depth of emotion, particularly in the beautiful woodwind passages. Lloyd does not dally and therefore achieves music of great depth without being sentimental. A March then follows, which gives the third movement a feeling of finality. This is only dispelled when the fourth and last movement appears. After a mysterious opening, the movement, marked Andante con Malinconico, builds to several controlled climaxes with music that seems to be trying to break free. There are many passages where both brass and woodwind predominate. The work ends on a quiet, mysterious note. In this work Lloyd was experimenting with polytonality, in order to give dramatic effect. Even allowing for revision, this work demonstrates a considerable advance over the First Symphony.

The Third Symphony, perhaps, gives the listener the best idea of Lloyd's early, distinctive style. It was written in 1933 and first performed, at the instigation of John Ireland, in 1935, in London, by the BBC Symphony Orchestra with the composer conducting. This twenty-three minute work uses the same instrumentation as the First Symphony, at times revealing a greater depth of emotion which anticipates Lloyd's later works.

The opening Allegro con Fuoco soon provides the glorious 'big tune', which slips quietly into the Lento. It is in the second movement's quieter moments that a greater depth of emotion is revealed and which rivals Lloyd's later works. This movement starts with a mysterious feel and, as it progresses, becomes menacing, before building to a climax. The movement ends quietly. The Finale, marked Energico, opens with a brilliant fanfare that one feels would not be out of place in one of Lloyd's operas. The brass eventually dies away and allows the rest of the orchestra to continue with a theme played mainly by strings. This is followed by a quieter woodwind passage before the brass return to the fore in a triumphal coda.

Lloyd's second opera, The Serf, was first performed at the Royal Opera House, Covent Garden, in 1938, conducted by Albert Coates. This opera is set in the Hambleton Hills on the edge of the North Yorkshire Moors following the Norman Conquest and concerns ill-fated peasant lovers, Sigrid and Cerdic, who are pursued by the son of their feudal Lord. The libretto was again by Lloyd's father, William. Despite critical praise, Lloyd did not consider it a success saying, 'Albert Coates, who had been a great conductor, was deteriorating rapidly and he made a frightful mess of it. It drove me out of the theatre, actually.' Lloyd thought highly enough of the music to draw two orchestral suites from the opera.

The Second World War Lloyd enlist in the Royal Marines and, as a bandsman, was on his ship, HMS Trinidad, moored at Scapa Flow in 1941 when the Bandmaster requested he write a march for the newly commissioned ship. Unfortunately the Captain was a friend of Vaughan Williams and had requested a march from that composer. The problem was only solved when the Captain decided to hold a competition on deck for the crew to choose which of the two marches should be used. The Lloyd march won. Lloyd later arranged the HMS Trinidad March for brass band. A version for full orchestra was premiered at the 2013 Last Night of the Proms, receiving an enthusiastic response.

Lloyd's Symphony No.4 was the work that brought the composer back to composition, written as it was under great mental and physical stress following his war injuries. It was written in 1945/46 in Switzerland where he went with his wife Nancy to convalesce. Writing only a few bars at a time, he managed to complete this symphony, which was not only the longest to date, but also the one that touched on his deepest feelings.

This symphony uses larger forces than the first three and has an Allegro Moderato that combines music of turmoil with foreboding passages and interludes of tragic isolation. The composer has identified this movement with the storms and darkness of his war experiences. The second movement Lento Tranquillo, has the composer remembering the peacefulness of a past journey up the Norwegian coast. Any such peacefulness seems to be viewed through the eyes of one who has suffered appallingly and there is a tragically cold and distant feeling to this music. A warmer passionate note becomes more obvious nearer the end, and it closes with some tranquillity. The Scherzo of the third movement is the first sign of a lightening of mood with music that is almost balletic in nature. Lloyd has said very little concerning the finale, simply that it is similar to the old convention of playing quick, cheerful tunes after the funeral. There is, of course, much more to the music, which is marked Lento - Allegro ma non Troppo. Lloyd always tried to search for the 'light at the end of the tunnel' despite whatever tragic events were in his mind.

The Fourth Symphony, not performed until 1981 when taken up by the Cheltenham Festival, ranks as one of the composer's finest works, and, I believe, his first mature symphony.

Lloyd's next symphony, his Symphony No.5, may be lighter in mood, but at little under an hour it is a large work. Written in 1948, whilst still convalescing in Switzerland, the Fifth Symphony reflects the happier mood brought about by staying on the edge of Lake Neuchatel. George and Nancy Lloyd found rooms on top of a barn with an extra room for the composer to work. The glorious hot summer in this idyllic location, together with his improving health, brought about this new work.

The first movement, marked Pastorale Allegretto con Tenerezza, shows at once a relaxed and sunny mood. Brass and percussion are not used. Notwithstanding this, there are still quiet moments of reflection. The second movement, marked Grave, opens with the brass that are missing in the first. The music then quietens to a hymn like tune with occasional interruptions from the brass. Violins and violas are not used. As the movement progresses, the brass become more involved in the steady 'hymn tune'. As the music rises to a climax, the brass again become dominant, with an insistent underlying drum beat, but at the last they drop back again. The following Rondo has a delicate bubbling dancing theme. The strings have only the horns and one trumpet to accompany them, together with the woodwind.

The emotional core of the work is the fourth movement Lamento. This movement, the longest of all, uses the full orchestra. After a brief introduction, a clarinet plays a tune that predominates, a theme of heartfelt anguish. Lloyd himself spoke of its "…dark, rich, tragic colour…" "its cry of despair …" Several times it tries to shake off this mood, only to fall back into deeper and colder despair. This movement ends quietly without any sense of overcoming the feeling of desolation. If the composer was finding ease from his appalling war experiences, then it is obvious that such ghosts were never far away. The finale, marked Vivace, brings about a complete contrast with music of great colour and vitality. The second subject is announced on the woodwind, passed onto the strings and then carried around the whole orchestra.

The sheer joy of writing for full orchestra with such flair, panache and colour was probably not repeated until the Eighth Symphony, written in 1961. The skilful orchestration would be remarkable from any composer, let alone one still recovering from such injuries. The end is truly triumphant.

Lloyd's importance in contemporary British music in the immediate post war era is demonstrated by the fact that, in 1949, three composers were commissioned to write an opera for the Festival of Britain in 1951. Vaughan Williams provided his long gestated Pilgrim's Progress, Benjamin Britten provided Billy Budd and George Lloyd wrote his third opera John Socman for the Carla Rosa Opera Company, the principal touring company of that time.

The subject of John Socman seems appropriate too; an archer returning from Agincourt to reclaim his lover, who has, whilst he was away, been taken by John Socman. Despite another enthusiastic audience reception, George felt strongly that the circumstances of the production of John Socman had made a travesty of his opera. Yet in this opera one can hear a strength and confidence that seems new to his music. Despite this, it was the circumstances of the production of John Socman combined with the death of his father that drove Lloyd to give up music and move to the Dorset countryside to run a nursery. He vowed never to enter an opera house again.

The musical climate was also not particularly conducive to tonal music with the rise of modernism. Lloyd had studied serial music but simply didn't like it. It was against this prevailing attitude that Lloyd's music would have to compete in the decades to come. He had never intended to become a symphonist. It's true that, before the war, he had written three symphonies but his true love was opera. It was only circumstances that changed his direction.

During the twenty years that George Lloyd and his wife Nancy lived at Ryewater in Dorset, he wrote four symphonies. The first work to be written at Ryewater was the Sixth Symphony from 1956. A gap of some eight years had separated Lloyd's Fifth and Sixth symphonies. Eventually, he had begun to compose again, often rising early to write his music before the day's business. Lloyd's intention for this symphony was to write a work that was "... concise, bright and lively ... music that sings ..." The first movement certainly fulfils this intention with music of substance but yet with a motion that sounds remarkably relaxed, given the composer's state of health. The following Adagio has a simplicity that belies its melancholic nature. When the first tune returns, after a central section, it is just as restrained as before. The finale, marked Vivace, starts with a wonderfully light touch with pizzicato strings and flute flourishes, followed by jaunty, yet more rapid flute passages. A short reflective section leads to a noisy, jolly conclusion with brass in full evidence. It is easy to overlook the qualities of this twenty-three minute symphony.

The Seventh Symphony, arguably his finest, was written between 1957 and 1959. If Lloyd's Sixth Symphony was generally a lighter and happier work, the Seventh must rank as his most pessimistic.

The composer tells us that this symphony was written with the story of Proserpine in his mind and that Greek legends were translated by him into psychological or spiritual states. The symphony certainly seems to contain some of Lloyd's most painful experiences in its three movements.

The first movement commences with a dark and mysterious theme interspersed with a lighter note. The composer tells us that this shows the joyful side of Proserpine, although the music never seems to shake off the darker elements. The music contains some of the composer's most colourful orchestration. The movement ends quietly, with a three-note motif that anticipates the opening of the next movement.

Lloyd heads the score in the second movement with a quote from Swinburne's poem "The Garden of Proserpine."

'Pale, beyond porch and portal,
Crowned with calm leaves, she stands
Who gathers all things mortal
With cold immortal hands.'

With this movement, we are now back in the cold, emotionally frozen world of the Fourth Symphony. Yet here, the grief seems even more hopeless. As the music progresses, it warms and becomes slightly less pessimistic. Here there are beautiful passages for flute and wonderfully rich writing for the lower strings.

The third movement opens loudly with percussion, brass and strings and, in the composer's words, concerns the desperate side of life. He quotes again from Swinburne.

'And all dead years draw thither,
And all disastrous things;
Dead dreams that snows have shaken,

Wild leaves that winds have taken,
Red strays of ruined springs.'

Lloyd certainly had cause to reflect on the words in this quote. Only the overwhelming need to compose caused such emotion to be allowed a voice in this symphony. As the movement progresses, it slowly builds from peak to peak, before the climactic outburst from the full orchestra. The music subsides and the symphony ends quietly, with a despondency rare in this composer's music.

To read the whole of Swinburne's poem, "The Garden of Proserpine", perhaps enables one to understand more fully the feelings in the composer's mind when he wrote the Seventh Symphony or, alternatively, one can sit back and allow the powerful, emotional and stunningly written symphony to speak for itself.

It was Lloyd's intention, with his Eighth Symphony (1961), to write a brilliant and colourful work, something he certainly achieved in the first and last movements of this three movement work. Some commentators have seen in the second movement, memories of past tragedy and the recollection of the composer's wartime experiences. Certainly, the music seems to be reflecting on some great sorrow, but the composer gives no indication as to the nature of this sadness.

After a quiet, Tranquillo, opening, the brass heralds the quickening of tempo, whereby the music builds up the Allegro in stages until the listener arrives at a broad, sweeping theme on the horns. The pace slackens from time to time with some beautiful woodwind passages, but the brass calls the orchestra back to the broad sweeping theme which, in many ways, gives the impression of the rugged sweep of the West Country coast. As the movement progresses, climax builds on climax as the broad sweeping nature of the music develops. As the movement draws to a close, the music quietens and ends with tranquillity.

After a quiet opening, the Largo strengthens with strange, swirling sounds in the orchestra. The music falls away to quieter passages but is interrupted by an angry outburst from the brass. There follows the main theme on the clarinets, then the strings. Here the music has a grief that is unbearable. There are further outbursts from the brass but with each return of the main theme, the anguish increases. There is a sense of resignation as the movement closes quietly.

The finale, Vivace, gives no doubt as to its purpose to shed all sad thoughts and begins in lively fashion, positively dancing along. Even in the quieter moments, there is no hint of gloom. Apart from a short reflective passage towards the end, the pace does not slacken and, indeed, increases right up to the end.

This was the symphony that brought about a renewed interest in Lloyd's music. He had made friends with John Ogdon who, in 1969, managed to 'slip the scores of two symphonies through the door' of the BBC, one of which was the Eighth Symphony. Nevertheless, it still took some eight years before it was performed, in 1977, by the BBC Northern Symphony Orchestra conducted by Edward Downes.

Lloyd's four piano concertos come from his time at Ryewater as does his first violin concerto. Lloyd was already thinking of writing a piano concerto when he heard the playing of John Ogdon, at that time one of Britain's most promising and interesting younger pianists. Lloyd kept Ogdon's playing in mind as he wrote his single movement Piano Concerto No.1 'Scapegoat' in 1962/63.

If further proof was needed that Lloyd's music was not stuck in some past generation then it is this work that has an improvisatory feel and, part way through, the feel of jazz variations. Nevertheless this is a work that is at turns tragic and light-hearted. There are so many colours and shadings in the orchestral part that make it as important as the piano part. Lloyd intended to write a three movement work but the initial material worked itself into a single movement concerto.

This remarkable work was first performed in October 1964 by John Ogdon with the Royal Liverpool Philharmonic Orchestra conducted by Sir Charles Groves. This led to a friendship with Ogdon with Lloyd helping the pianist with the orchestration of some his own compositions.

Having a slow movement and a finale left over from the First Piano concerto, Lloyd went ahead, in 1964, with writing another first movement to go with them, but this material developed into another single movement concerto, the Piano Concerto No.2. It was Martin Roscoe who gave the first performance of this work and, indeed, went on to record both the first and second piano concertos. This first performance was given with the BBC Philharmonic Orchestra conducted by Edward Downes in May 1984.

Lloyd's spare slow movement and finale for a piano concerto did not go to waste as, when he sat down to write a first movement for his Piano Concerto No.3, in 1967/68 the material co-operated and became the first movement to which the two spare movements were added. This concerto was first performed in 1988, by Kathryn Stott and the BBC Philharmonic Orchestra conducted by the composer in a recording for Albany Records.

Lloyd's Piano Concerto No.4 from 1970 was the first to be recorded, again by Kathryn Stott with the London Symphony Orchestra conducted by the composer, in 1987. Stott and the LSO had already performed the work with the composer again conducting at a concert given at the Royal Festival Hall, London in 1984.

A critic once asked the question, in relation to this concerto, 'when is a piano concerto not a piano concerto?' When does it become merely piano obligato or a concertante work? Lloyd's fourth concerto is no less a concerto just because his brilliant orchestral writing has a significant role, with the piano taking more of an equal role at times. The first movement again has jazz like influences and the second movement shows quite advanced tendencies in the occasional chamber like writing and dissonance between instruments and, indeed, its somewhat diffuse sounds.

Although the 1960s saw Lloyd turning his attention to piano works, his Ninth Symphony came in 1969. Many composers have felt overshadowed by Beethoven's Ninth Symphony, but in his Ninth, Lloyd said simply that he solved the problem by writing a twenty-eight minute light-hearted work, an approach often taken by other 20th century composers with the same problem.

The first movement opens with an Allegro, which has a very light touch and feel to it, whilst also allowing moments of melancholy. There is a beautiful passage for clarinet, the theme then being passed around the orchestra and after a return to the opening theme, builds to a climax with the full orchestra. The movement ends quietly with a solo violin against a background of hushed strings.

The opening of the second movement, marked Largo, has menacing brass chords, which settle down to a tranquil theme. The dissonant chords return louder and are followed by more desperate desolation. Lloyd conjures up emotions of searing intensity in this music. Towards the end, the brass discords return with even more intensity, the movement ending quietly.

The finale, marked Allegro con Brio, starts with a misleadingly abstract theme on percussion before quickly building up to the main theme for full orchestra. There is some wonderful writing for brass that makes this some of the most optimistic music written by Lloyd. The glorious end is riotously brilliant.

Lloyd does not say a great deal about his Ninth Symphony, only that the first movement is about a young girl dancing, the second concerns the grief stricken remembrances of an old lady and the third a merry-go-round that keeps going round and round. When listening to this symphony, it is impossible not to speculate on Lloyd's own emotional identity with grief.

This surprisingly fertile musical period for Lloyd also brought his first major orchestral work Charade (1969). In many ways Charade shows a sign of Lloyd's improving health particularly if one looks at some of the titles of the movements such as Student Power, LSD, Flying Saucers and Party Politics, which give a clue to his sense of humour and, yes, sometimes, cynicism. Certainly it is very much a 60's piece showing Lloyd's view of the world and his forward looking writing.

The violin was, of course, very much Lloyd's instrument, having studied, in his youth, under Albert Sammons. His war injuries prevented him from playing his violin, believed to be one of two owned by Lady Hamilton, for many years. There is a singing quality that shows itself in the two Violin Concertos of 1970 and 1977. There is no doubt of the dominance of the soloist in these two works. The Concerto No.1 for Violin and Strings (1970) is very much in the tradition of 20th century string works with a very affecting third movement Largo. The Concerto No.2 for Violin and Winds (1977) again produced a distinctive sound, particularly in the second movement, showing how Lloyd was always looking to expand his palette.

This reawakened interest in the violin brought two chamber works; in 1975, Lament, Air and Dance for violin and piano and, in 1976, the Sonata for Violin and Piano. Both reveal a distinctive violin sound in their writing where the instrument is always allowed to sing though. Intercom Baby was also originally for violin in the1970s but transcribed for piano in 1987.

In 1966 Lloyd had written An African Shrine for John Ogdon. The 1970s brought even more piano works with some pretty unusual titles, The Road through Samarkand (1972), St Anthony and the Bogside Beggar (1972), The Aggressive Fishes (1972), The Lilyleaf and the Grasshopper (1972) and The Transformation of that Naked Ape (1972), all wonderfully descriptive pieces.

The Lilyleaf and the Grasshopper is a beautifully written piece, very descriptive and, indeed, rather French in sound. For a composer who stated that the piano was not his instrument, this is a spectacularly fine work.

Aubade for two pianos came in 1971 but had to wait until 1996 to be recorded. The author and his wife had got to know pianist, Caroline Clemmow, who performs with her husband Anthony Goldstone as a piano duo. This led to Caroline and Tony Goldstone recording the work for Albany Records. Aubade is another fine work inspired by that dream like state when we are just awakening. Interestingly one of the characters who appears is Lady Hamilton playing her violin.

If opera was no longer a viable project for Lloyd then surely The Vigil of Venus, from 1979/80, is his most operatic work, perhaps fulfilling his need to write in an operatic way. With the Vigil of Venus, Lloyd had hoped for a Proms performance but had to wait for a Festival Hall performance some nine years later. Indeed, the difficulties in achieving a performance were given in a letter from Lloyd to the author dated 25th June 1989 when he wrote '...Now let me give you some good news about the Vigil of Venus. It was going to be played at the Kennedy Centre, Washington and then recorded at Troy in April...this all fell through...very soon after that Decca became interested and finally set up a whole new project together with the Welsh National opera. The piece will be performed at the Festival Hall on the 7th November this year and recorded in Wales...' Some critics drew attention to a perceived lack of variety in the work but, given the texts, Lloyd appropriately gives us a suitably buoyant, Italianate piece, full of life, with some gloriously operatic writing.

At the premiere Lloyd conducted the Orchestra and Chorus of Welsh National Opera with the soloists Carolyn James and Thomas Booth, going on to record the work with the same forces for Decca the following November at the Brangwyn Hall, Swansea.

There was to be a gap of thirteen years before, in 1982, Lloyd wrote his Symphony No.10. A sign of the increasing interest in Lloyd's music, this new symphony was commissioned by the BBC and first performed by the Northern Brass Ensemble. It is written for thirteen brass players. Lloyd's enthusiasm for brass writing comes as no surprise given the works that would be written for brass band during this decade. What is surprising is the range of colours and textures that are achieved in this strikingly original work, subtitled 'November Journeys' and referring to journeys made by the composer to various English Cathedrals. Nevertheless, the music isn't, nor is it intended to be, ecclesiastical.

The opening Allegro Moderato contains a jaunty theme given richness and variety by different combinations of brass. Here, it seems, is the happy traveller on his journey. The second movement, marked Calma, gives the feeling of the timelessness of a great cathedral, by its gentle and quiet delicacy. The music rises to a gentle yet glorious climax, the majestic grandeur of a great building, before ending quietly.

The following Andante, with its economical use of the various brass instruments, amazes the listener with the diversity and richness of scoring. The opening theme is interrupted at intervals by more complex passages before ending quietly. The listener is given the impression of the traveller wandering around the cathedral and stopping periodically and could perhaps be equated with Mussorgsky's 'Pictures at an Exhibition', in the way that the traveller 'promenades.'

The final movement, marked Energico, begins with a fanfare-like motif that develops into the main theme. There is a momentary interruption in the middle of the movement where there follows another fanfare. The music then becomes somewhat mysterious and quiet but soon rises to a climax, before dropping back to a quiet close, only interrupted by two short outbursts, where it ends.

In this symphony Lloyd showed, if such was still necessary, his masterly skills as an orchestrator. This combined with his ability to create endless melodic invention resulted in an outstanding work.

In the 1980's Lloyd's increasing interest in music for brass brought forth A Miniature Triptych (1981), Royal Parks (1985), Diversions on a Bass Theme (1986) and English Heritage (1988) many commissioned as test pieces for brass band competitions. Lloyd's enthusiasm was such that he very much endeared himself to those involved in these competitions, always determined never to miss a performance. His work for wind band, The Forest of Arden, written in 1987, was commissioned by BASBWE (British Association of Symphonic Bands and Wind Ensembles). In 1993 Lloyd would go on to write another brass band work, Kings Messenger, for the Swiss National Brass Band Competition in Montreux.

Lloyd was always seeking new sounds, something which tempted him to write another symphony in order to, in his own words "...

once more extend a little further the range of sounds I had already been making ..."

This he achieved in his Symphony No.11 (1985), which was commissioned by the Albany Symphony Orchestra. President of the Albany Symphony Orchestra, Peter Kermani, heard the BBC broadcast of Lloyd's Symphony No. 8 which resulted in a commission for the Eleventh Symphony. It was premiered at the concert hall of the Troy Savings Bank, New York State on 31st October 1986, receiving a standing ovation.

Lasting some sixty minutes, this symphony has five movements. The opening movement, Vivo, uses the large orchestra, bigger than that used in the Fourth Symphony, to full effect. But as with much of Lloyd's output, volume of sound isn't everything. The orchestra soon drops to a quiet, mysterious passage for woodwind, strings and percussion. The following climaxes soon drop back to quietness whilst still revealing a nervous energy. It is this wonderful use of small sections of the orchestra to achieve a variety of colours that marks out Lloyd as the superb orchestrator that he is. As the movement ends quietly, the listener is surprised to notice that nearly one third of the symphony has elapsed, such is the attention held.

The following Lento uses the simplest of means, with strings and soft brass, to create a flowing melody with an underlying pulse that builds to a glorious climax.
After a fleeting dance-like third movement marked Leggiero e brillante, with its highly original middle section for woodwind and celeste, there follows a deeply felt fourth movement marked Grave. If the second movement's Lento showed in full Lloyd's lyrical gifts, then it is this movement that bears the emotional weight of the symphony. The brass takes a prominent role whilst the military sounds are reinforced by drums. The composer himself talks of "... the overtones of a military funeral..." Had he still failed to

completely purge the events of over forty years ago or had more recent events been in his mind? Towards the end of the movement, Lloyd still manages to lighten the mood.

A brass fanfare heralds the Finale, which moves ahead with a purpose, whilst allowing moments of quiet beauty. As with the previous movements, the listener is able to hear many quiet, subtle colourations, which are such a feature of this composer's music. The work ends with a massive and gloriously optimistic finale.

This symphony is a wonderful achievement, which reveals more with each hearing. In it, Lloyd has indeed managed, after ten previous symphonies, to write a work which is original and new. The coda gives a strong impression of being the final end. After this, Lloyd swore that he would write no more symphonies.

Other orchestral works followed, Dying Tree, written in 1992, given its World Premiere at the Barbican on 20th September 1994 and Floating Cloud, written and first performed in 1993, in Hong Kong, by the Hong Kong Philharmonic conducted by Lloyd.

Lloyd's association with the Albany Symphony Orchestra led to his becoming the orchestra's Artistic Advisor for two seasons, conducting works by other composers such as Sibelius, Dvorak, Verdi, Vaughan Williams, Delius, Randell Thompson, Copland, and Paul Creston and to the commissioning of another symphony, the Symphony No.12.

Lloyd had hinted at another symphony when he wrote to the author in December 1987 saying '...I swore that No.11 would be my last, but maybe I shall have to eat my words one day. Maybe just one more, but not like Myaskovsky --- no one can ever remember which is which!' On 24th October 1988 Lloyd confirmed this in another letter saying that '...yes, I am in the middle of a new symphony (this really is the last) which I am doing for the Albany S/O...'

In writing the Twelfth Symphony, the composer looked at the structure he had used for his First Symphony, some fifty-seven years previously. The Twelfth is in three sections and played without a break.

The first section consists of an introduction, quietly flowing music for strings and woodwind, and is followed by a set of variations, the first being an exquisite passage for flutes. The second variation dances along lightly until stopped by variation three, marked Grave. Such scoring, as in this section, shows Lloyd to be very much of the late 20th Century in his use of dissonance, subtle yet vital to the music. The variations finish with a march-like theme.

With the central section, marked Adagio, the listener comes to the emotional depth of the work. It is music of sensitivity and calm, as though the troubles of previous symphonies are over - a form of looking back, but not mere nostalgia. The many beauties of the orchestration would require an essay of their own. A tentative figure on strings, reinforced by the timpani, leads us into the third and final section, marked Allegro. After a short while the music picks up momentum and seems to have a natural drive, almost unstoppable in its climaxes.

The brass, one of Lloyd's distinctive fingerprints, has an important place in this section, giving some glorious sounds. The music slows and quietens towards the end and the listener hears magical sounds as the symphony comes to its serene conclusion.

The symphony, completed in 1989, was premiered by the Albany Symphony Orchestra in the Troy Savings Bank Music Hall, New York State, in March 1990. Lloyd wrote to the author to say '...we got home two days ago...No's 12 and 1 were duly recorded; the orchestra played well and we think the disc will prove to be the best we've done in the Troy Hall...'

Its UK premiere took place in August 1990 in Worcester Cathedral as part of the Three Choirs Festival after which Lloyd wrote to the author saying, '...yes, I feel a bit the same as you about last year. It was a special evening for me too; the sort that does not come often. There was an extraordinary atmosphere; perfect weather; as the sun began to lower after that scorching day I was outside beyond the East door waiting to conduct, the chorus voices came floating by, a perfect setting for Delius...I don't think I'll go back there; it could never be as good.' It was at that moment that Lloyd conceived the idea of his next choral work, A Symphonic Mass, written in 1992, a work that is arguably his masterpiece.

In the meantime, in 1990 came another orchestral work, not performed until 2013, Le Pont du Gard, inspired by the ancient Roman aqueduct that crosses the Gardon River in Vers-Pont-du-Gard near Remoulins, in southern France.

Of Lloyd's A Symphonic Mass Ivan March wrote in his review for the Gramophone magazine 'This in my view is one of the finest pieces of English choral writing of the twentieth century. Listening to it... is a very moving experience...I hope choral societies will take it up...' Commissioned by the Brighton Festival it received its premiere on 9th May 1993. Such was the impact of the work that, during rehearsals, staff at the Brighton Dome were seen to be stopped in their tracks by the composer's thrilling orchestral and choral climaxes.

It is interesting to note Lloyd's choice of music when he appeared on the BBC programme Desert Island Discs on 23rd April 1995. He chose Tchaikovsky's Violin Concerto, an excerpt from his own opera, John Socman, Berlioz's Symphony Fantastique, an excerpt from the finale of his own Fourth Symphony, the Quartet from

Verdi's Rigoletto, Schumann's Carnaval de Wien, Elgar's Symphony No.2 and of Bach's Jesu Joy of Man's Desiring, his single choice. His luxury was Romney's portrait of Lady Hamilton, an interesting choice given the provenance of his own violin.

The next major work to follow was A Litany written in 1995 and commissioned by the Guildford Choral Society, a setting of texts by John Donne and first performed on 16th March 1996. Described in the Gramophone as '…rich in colour and varied in resources…' Lloyd shows his tremendous skill in word setting, in texts that would not normally lend themselves to such use. That year Lloyd also produced two shorter works, Psalm 130 and Invocation to the Virgin Mary.

It was at the Barbican in 1994 that the author talked to Lloyd about whether he had ever considered writing a Cello Concerto. Nothing came of it then but maybe a seed was sown for in 1997 came his Cello Concerto. The score is inscribed with the words 'Have you no pity for those you would destroy?' Whether these reflected his wartime experiences or the years of struggle against the musical establishment of the time, one can never know. Suffice to say that, perhaps, Lloyd knew he was entering the last phase of his life and took the opportunity to vent his feelings. The work is not valedictory but reinforces the composer's resilience and hope, tinged with regret and loss. The concerto was completed in July 1997 but not recorded until three years after his death. This glorious, passionate work is one that should surely be in the repertoire.

Lloyd's Requiem, written in 1998, was given its first performance in Oxford on 17th October 1999. Commissioned by the Exon Singers the performance was given by them under their director Matthew Owens. In this work, gone is the colourful orchestral writing so familiar in Lloyd's music. Given his fragile health he knew he would not be able to complete a full orchestration. It is written for just countertenor, organ and choir. There are many fine moments in this work such as when the countertenor enters at the beginning of the Agnus Dei, one of Lloyd's most magical creations.

Lloyd once said that '…eventually composers will come round to meeting the public halfway…' There may be some resistance from certain critics today but the tide has begun to turn. Composers are now adopting styles which often combine modernist and melodic features and, in this post-modernist world, we can now see that he was absolutely right.

# Catalogue of Works

| OPERAS | Date Written | Date first Performed | Artists & Venue | Conductor |
|---|---|---|---|---|
| Iernin | 1933-34 | 1934 (amateur) 1935 (pro) | Penzance Lyceum Theatre London | George Lloyd George Lloyd |
| The Serf | 1936-38 | 1938 | Royal Opera House Covent Garden | Albert Coates |
| John Socman | 1949-51 | 1951 | Carl Rosa Opera Company, Bristol | Arthur Hammond |

| CONCERTOS | Date Written | Date first Performed | Artists & Venue | Conductor |
|---|---|---|---|---|
| Piano No. 1 Scapegoat | 1962 – 1963 | 1964 | John Ogden RLPO, Liverpool | Charles Groves |
| Piano No. 2 | 1964 | 1983 | Martin Roscoe BBC Philharmonic Manchester | Edward Downes |
| Piano No. 3 | 1967 – 1968 | 1988 | Kathryn Stott BBC Philharmonic Manchester | George Lloyd |
| Piano No. 4 | 1970 | 1984 | Kathryn Stott LSO Festival Hall, London | George Lloyd |

| | | | | |
|---|---|---|---|---|
| Violin No. 1 | 1970 | 1998 (recorded) | Cristina Anghelescu Philharmonia Orchestra Henry Wood Hall | David Parry |
| Violin No. 2 | 1977 | 1986 | Manoug Parikian BBC Philharmonic Manchester | George Lloyd |
| Cello | 1997 | 2000 | Alexander Baillie Orquestra Nacional do Porto, Portugal | Peter Marchbank |

| SYMPHONIES | Date Written | Date first Performed | Artists & Venue | Conductor |
|---|---|---|---|---|
| Symphony No. 1 | 1932 | 1933 | Penzance Orchestra St John's Hall Penzance | George Lloyd |
| Symphony No. 2 | 1933 | 1934 | Eastbourne Municipal Orchestra, Eastbourne | George Lloyd |
| Symphony No. 3 | 1933 | 1935 | BBC Symphony Orchestra, London | George Lloyd |
| Symphony No. 4 | 1945 – 1946 | 1981 | Philharmonia Orchestra Cheltenham Festival | Edward Downes |
| Symphony No. 5 | 1947 – 1948 | 1979 | Philharmonia Orchestra BBC Studio | Edward Downes |
| Symphony No. 6 | 1956 | 1980 | BBC Northern Symphony Orchestra Manchester | Edward Downes |
| Symphony No. 7 | 1957 – 1959 | 1979 | BBC Northern Symphony Orchestra Manchester | Edward Downes |

| | | | BBC Northern Symphony Orchestra Manchester | Edward Downes |
|---|---|---|---|---|
| Symphony No. 8 | 1961 | 1977 | BBC Northern Symphony Orchestra Manchester | Edward Downes |
| Symphony No. 9 | 1969 | 1982 | BBC Philharmonic Orchestra Manchester | Edward Downes |
| Symphony No. 10 | 1982 | 1982 | Northern Brass Ensemble Manchester | Edward Downes |
| Symphony No. 11 | 1985 | 1986 | Albany Symphony Orchestra, Troy, USA | George Lloyd |
| Symphony No. 12 | 1989 | 1990 | Albany Symphony Orchestra, Troy, USA | George Lloyd |

| MISC ORCHESTRAL | Date Written | Date first Performed | Artists & Venue | Conductor |
|---|---|---|---|---|
| HMS Trinidad March (orch. version) | 1941 | 2013 | BBC Symphony Orchestra - BBC Proms (Last Night) | Marin Alsop |
| Overture – The Serf | 1947 | 1948 | Radio Orchestra, Festival of Anglo-French Music Marseilles | Pierre Monier |
| Overture -John Socman | 1951 | 1951 | Carl Rosa Opera Company, Bristol | Arthur Hammond |
| Charade - suite | 1969 | 1992 | BBC Philharmonic Royal Northern College of Music | George Lloyd |
| Floating Cloud | 1993 | 1993 | Hong Kong Philharmonic | George Lloyd |
| Dying Tree | 1992 | 1994 | Bournemouth Symphony Orchestra, Barbican | George Lloyd |
| Le Pont du Gard | 1990 | 2014 | Bath Philharmonia London (recording) | Jason Thornton |

| | | | | |
|---|---|---|---|---|
| Suites No. 1 & 2 The Serf | 1997 | Suite No. 1 2001 | Albany Symphony Orchestra (recording) | David Alan Miller |
| Prelude Act II The Serf | 1936-1938 | 1938 | Royal Opera House Covent Garden | Albert Coates |
| In Memoriam (orch. version) | 1996 | 2014 | Bath Philharmonia London (recording) | Jason Thornton |

| CHORAL | Date Written | Date first Performed | Artists & Venue | Conductor |
|---|---|---|---|---|
| The Vigil of Venus | 1979 - 1980 | 1989 | Welsh National Opera, Festival Hall, London | George Lloyd |
| A Symphonic Mass | 1992 | 1993 | Bournemouth SO Brighton Festival Chorus Brighton | George Lloyd |
| A Litany | 1995 | 1996 | Guildford Choral Society Janice Watson, David Wilson Johnson, Philharmonia Orchestra | George Lloyd |
| Psalm 130 | 1995 | | The Tippett Choir | Mr J D Owens |
| Invocation to the Virgin Mary | 1995 | | | |
| Requiem Mass | 1998 | 2000 | Steven Watson Exon Singers Oxford | Matthew Owens |

| BRASS | Date Written | Date first Performed | Artists & Venue | Conductor |
|---|---|---|---|---|
| HMS Trinidad March | 1941 | 1941 | Band of HMS Trinidad, Scapa Flow, Orkney | |
| Royal Parks | 1984 | 1985 | European Brass Band Competition Copenhagen | |
| Diversions on a Bass Theme | 1986 | 1986 | Mineworkers National Brass Band Competition Blackpool | |
| English Heritage | 1987 | 1988 | Black Dyke & Brighouse Brass Bands, Kenwood | Geoffrey Brand |
| King's Messenger | 1993 | 1994 | Swiss National Brass Band Competition, Montreux | |
| Evening Song | 1951 | 1991 | Black Dyke Mills Brass Band, Dewsbury | David King |
| Forest of Arden | 1987 | 1988 | Solihull | |
| A Miniature Triptych | 1981 | 1982 | Equale Brass, Malvern Festival | |

| INSTRUMENTAL | Date Written | Date first performed | Artists |
|---|---|---|---|
| Aubade for 2 Pianos | 1971 | Recorded in 1996 | Caroline Clemmow & Anthony Goldstone |
| Extracts from The Serf for Violin & Piano | 1974 | | |
| Lament, Air & Dance for Violin & Piano | 1975 | Recorded in 1990 | Tasmin Little & Martin Roscoe |
| Sonata for Violin & Piano | 1976 | Recorded in 1990 | Tasmin Little & Martin Roscoe |
| The Road through Samarkand - piano | 1972 | Recorded in 1988 | Martin Roscoe |
| The Road through Samarkand - 2 pianos | 1995 | Recorded in 1996 | Caroline Clemmow & Anthony Goldstone |
| St Anthony & the Bogside Beggar - piano | 1972 | Recorded in 1988 | Martin Roscoe |
| The Aggressive Fishes - piano | 1972 | Recorded in 1988 | Martin Roscoe |
| Intercom Baby originally for violin - transcribed for piano | Late 1970s 1987 | Recorded in 1988 | Martin Roscoe |
| The Lilyleaf & the Grasshopper – piano | 1972 | Recorded in 1988 | Kathryn Stott |
| Transformation of that Naked Ape – piano | 1972 | Recorded in 1988 | Kathryn Stott |
| Eventide – piano | | Recorded in 1996 | Caroline Clemmow & Anthony Goldstone |
| Songs | Various | | |

# Discography

## OPERA

| Iernin | TROY 121/122/123 | BBC Concert Orchestra BBC Concert Singers George Lloyd |
|---|---|---|
| John Socman (highlights) | TROY 131 | Thomas Booth Janice Watson Philharmonia Orch London Voices, George Lloyd |

## SYMPHONIES

| Symphonies 1 & 12 | TROY 032 | Albany Symphony Orchestra Lloyd |
|---|---|---|
| Symphonies 2 & 9 | TROY 055 | BBC Philharmonic Orchestra Lloyd |
| Symphony 3 & Charade | TROY 090 | BBC Philharmonic Orchestra Lloyd |
| Symphony 4 | AR002 | Albany Symphony Orchestra Lloyd |
| Symphonies 4, 5 & 8 | Lyrita SRCD 2258 | Philharmonia Orchestra Downes |
| Symphony 5 | TROY 022 | BBC Philharmonic Orchestra Lloyd |
| Symphony 6 & 10 | TROY 015 | BBC Philharmonic Orch Philharmonic Brass, Lloyd |
| Symphony 7 | TROY 057 | BBC Philharmonic Orchestra Lloyd |
| Symphony 8 | TROY 230 | BBC Philharmonic Orchestra Lloyd |
| Symphony 11 | TROY 060 | Albany Symphony Orchestra Lloyd |

## CONCERTOS

| Piano Concerto 1 & 2 | TROY 037 | Martin Roscoe/BBC Philharmonic/Lloyd |
|---|---|---|
| Piano Concerto No.3 | TROY 019 | Kathryn Stott/ BBC Philharmonic/Lloyd |
| Piano Concerto No.4 | AR004 | Kathryn Stott/LSO/Lloyd |
| Violin Concerto No.1 & No.2 | TROY 316 | Cristina Anghelescu Philharmonia Orch/David Parry |
| Cello Concerto | TROY 458 | Anthony Ross/Albany Symphony Orchestra/ David Alan Miller |

## MISCELLANEOUS ORCHESTRAL

| HMS Trinidad March (orch. version) | EMR CD026 | Bath Philharmonia/ Jason Thornton |
|---|---|---|
| Overture - John Socman | TROY 015 | BBC Philharmonic Orchestra/Lloyd |
| Charade | TROY 090 | BBC Philharmonic Orchestra/Lloyd |
| In Memoriam (orch. version) | EMR CD026 | Bath Philharmonia/ Jason Thornton |
| Prelude to Act II of The Serf | EMR CD026 | Bath Philharmonia/ Jason Thornton |
| Serf Suite No.1 | TROY 458 | Albany Symphony Orchestra /David Alan Miller |
| Le Pont Du Gard | EMR CD026 | Bath Philharmonia/ Jason Thornton |

## BRASS

| | | |
|---|---|---|
| Royal Parks<br>Diversions on a Bass<br>Theme<br>English Heritage<br>Evening Song<br>HMS Trinidad March | TROY 051 | John Foster Black Dyke<br>Mills Band/David King |

## CHORAL

| | | |
|---|---|---|
| The Vigil of Venus | TROY 170 | Thomas Booth, Carolyn James<br>- Welsh National Opera/Lloyd |
| A Symphonic Mass | TROY 100 | Bournemouth SO, Brighton<br>Festival Chorus, Lloyd |
| A Litany | TROY 200 | Janice Watson,<br>Jeremy White<br>Guildford Choral Society<br>Philharmonia Orchestra/Lloyd |
| Requiem and<br>Psalm 130 | TROY 450 | Steven Wallace, Exon Singers<br>Matthew Owens |

## INSTRUMENTAL

| | | |
|---|---|---|
| Aubade for 2 Pianos<br>Eventide<br>The Road through<br>Samarkand (2 pianos) | TROY 248 | Anthony Goldstone &<br>Caroline<br>Clemmow |
| Lament, Air & Dance<br>Sonata for Violin & Piano | TROY 029 | Tasmin Little & Martin<br>Roscoe |
| Intercom Baby<br>The Aggressive Fishes<br>An African Shrine<br>The Road through<br>Samarkand<br>St Anthony & the Bogside<br>Beggar | AR003 | Martin Roscoe |
| The Lilyleaf & the<br>Grasshopper<br>Transformation of that<br>Naked Ape | AR004 | Kathryn Stott |

www.ingramcontent.com/pod-product-compliance
Lightning Source LLC
Chambersburg PA
CBHW072300170526
45158CB00003BA/1127